Poems from Paradise

Poems from Paradise

Wendy Barker

WordTech Editions

Published by WordTech Editions
P.O. Box 541106
Cincinnati, OH 45254-1106

Typeset in Lucida and Iowan Old Style by WordTech
Communications LLC, Cincinnati, OH

ISBN: 1932339892
LCCN: 2004115693

Poetry Editor: Kevin Walzer
Business Editor: Lori Jareo

Visit us on the web at www.wordtechweb.com

Acknowledgements

I am grateful to the editors of the following journals, in whose pages many of these poems first appeared, at times in different versions:

Borderlands: "To Reconstruct," "So This," "But I Couldn't,"
    "And Here," and "The Return"
The Brownstone Review: "The Rocks, " "Maybe I Listened," and
    "I Think"
The Connecticut Poetry Review: "Our Small" and "Oh, You Said,
    Your"
Midwest Poetry Review: "This Fence"
the new renaissance: "If I Could Shake"
Nimrod: International Journal: "You Standing" and "We Are"
Painted Bride Quarterly: "Through"
Poet Lore: "Bare," "Lemon, Oak, Cypress," and "Surrounded"
Poetry Kanto: "The Snow," "The Third Week," and "I Had
    Wanted to Say"
The Quest: An International Literary Journal (India): "Coloring"
    and "Sometimes"
The Spoon River Poetry Review: "The Divide" and "The Fifth
    Day"
Tex!: "In This Rain," "Pine," and "Evening"
The Toronto Review of Contemporary Writing Abroad: "You," "You
    Looked," and "If I Was the One"
White Heron: "Gift" and "The Pool"

I also wish to thank Sudeep Sen and Aark Arts Press in London, for publishing some of these poems in chapbook form (as *Eve Remembers*); the Rockefeller Foundation and the Villa Serbelloni at Bellagio, as well as the University of Texas at San Antonio, for space and time; Brenda Claiborne, Kevin Clark, Beverly Davis, David Dooley, Sandra M. Gilbert, Sharon Ankrum, Paulette Jiles, Jeannine Keenan, Christine Dumaine Leche, Sherry McKinney, Alicia Ostriker, and Hannah Stein, for care and sustenance; Amritjit Singh and

Saranindranath Tagore, for the challenges of translation; and, finally, Steven G. Kellman.

Table of Contents

I

I Don't Know

where you came from.
Always, you were there.

Our steps, easy, even
on the narrowest

paths. Your back, hip,
moving, mine.

The Fifth Day

I found fruit, red, and
freckled, small

under their pleated
leaves. I almost missed them.

Wanted to show you.
The pleasure of watching

you eat them too—
little sweetnesses.

Lemon, Oak, Cypress

But there were so many others,
leaves like new lace,
fine crochet, and so many
kinds of seeds—round, like bells,
butterflies, or birds' wings.
And the trees with the big leaves,
the leaves, like your hands.

The Third Week

I noticed the orchids,
petals, calyx, and called,
and you said yes, yes,
but it was the water you saw,
streams, both sides of the path.

What you loved—and what
we looked at for a long
time—was the dark water
beside the pale orchids,
the steady, even flow of it.

Oh, You Said, Your

fingers and half-open
mouth pressing bits of me

I had thought were ordinary,
separate pieces of my body,

till they began to swim
together with your hands.

Our Small

touching. Breezes. I turned
my palm. You stroked

a leaf, cup, widening
lake, the shuddering tree.

At First You Insisted

it wasn't passion
the way we fell
silent, alongside

silences deepening
the spaces among
damp leaves

till there was no
space anywhere
between us, light and

air my breasts, your hands,
our breath, our breath, our
unbroken breathing.

At Last

we swam in the lake
of each other. All night
the current washed

rocks from shore, eased
the jagged edges, dissolved
stones into silt

reaching under
the highest of tides,
entire body of water.

Butterfly

After, we lay still, our backs
in touch as if we had

become one body.
Our heads, knees resting

on the ground, leaned
to either side, wings readying

for the flight ahead.
We did not think in halves.

We Said

we wanted to cross the lake.
For something we could not

name. To push from the sway
of water. I don't remember

how we found ourselves, rocking
the stones on the other side.

If I Was the One

who took another
path I couldn't say.

Cries in the wind.
Blanks among trees.

The Divide

Where was that spot on the slope
we were both so silent, when

high over water, transparent,
the air wrapped us?

Now You Are

nowhere. I can't even
remember our

mouths, tongues:
petals, one full

rose opening
after light rain

and not yet
yanked from the plant.

I Had Wanted to Say

let it be a gentle leaving.
From the trees, a little shade,

dappling to shape our
walk—until we cleared

a path through brush,
thickets tangling in on me.

At the Gate

the steps
drop steep,
hard, force
the knee
to bend.
Again.
Narrow
for human
feet, easy
to fall.
The long
cold rain.

Surrounded

by snow. And black lines
of trees, limbs, stumps.
Unsteady footing.
Whichever way I set out
to find you I will sink.

The Snow

You could not follow me.
Bare spots among rocks.

I have left the sloping
hills with their lilies

and lakesides, your body
a living stem. I am

winding through mountains.
Sleet as I leave.

This Fence

goes on forever. Stones,
markers, set as if
on graves, but graves
placed close, touching.

Away

Wind shifts, grasses
bend to each other, away
from each other. You are so
far from me, even the trees blur.

I Have Become

imperceptible
as dry seed scattered,
cast from familiar
ground, wisp in air.

Bare

stretches of earth worked over,
fought over. Crops of rapeseed.
Stones in the walls are missing.
I have forgotten
the language of the field.

The Rocks

of this house fit
one into one, bones

with no cartilage.
Weary of motion.

Months could pass until
I let the door swing.

Maybe I Listened

to your namings till
my body ached, hollowed.

Did you think me
a kind of drum

to announce your presence?
You wouldn't have known

me as a bell, tongue
swollen in silence.

Too Busy

for all that. Laying out lines.
Grids across the flattened dirt.
Separate plants for each square.

They must not meet across
these borders I will be sure
to maintain. High expectations.

Yields. I have no time for you.
Even if you walked right up
to the edge of my boundaries.

I Think

you never existed. I named
you into my life. Or you
named me till I was nothing

but a rib torn from your lungs.
And still this ache to slip back
into your body, breathe you.

Or I could give you one of
the bones lining my long chest.
More: come live in my marrow.

To Reconstruct

those paths would take more
than we may ever

learn to do. A dove
calls from a branch

I can't see. To rebuild
what we had. Softness of

mosses. Your turning
to me, offering. Silken

air, streams trembling.
The way the moon filled.

The Snake

uncoiled until
I reached for you.

A braid of us
pulled tight. That rope

swing we played on.
To save our lives.

Spiral. Hang by
a single thread.

But I Couldn't

leave this field to find you.
I know where the rocks lie.

Working around them
takes no thinking, familiar

granite angles.
Past any further step

earth may crumble
to a labyrinth of caves,

or worse, stretch so vast
beyond me, I'll vanish.

Whether

one of us breathed
the sky or skimmed

lake shimmer, we didn't
ask of light that wove us,

keel and pool, air
and water. We never

asked if one of us
was an illusion.

We lived as the calla
lily's tongue lies

embedded in the creamy
bloom, full sail.

The Pool

Small fish break the surface
but always I am waiting
for the deep-rooted lily
to bloom again, planted
so down in my silt.

You Looked

me to life. What you saw.
Apricot, cream, and blue
of the pool. Lavender.

I am not of those things
you do not see here
moving among leaves

and twigs, but if I were
to learn to cultivate
the vines in rows, I could

move into the open
furrows between, and from
a distance, you would find me.

You

missing, bone
hard the trees
seep their white
bloom through stem,
tendril, leaf.

And your beard:
light curling
through the sweet,
dark hair, all
blossoming.

How far do
these white clouds
reach, from here
to that place
you are now?

I Want

all the poppies to bloom
a carpet, bright bed where

you could lie down. And if
I knew where you traveled,

I would cross the river,
climb unraveled banks,

ravines thick with brambles,
and pick their fruit. You might

not know these tangled
arms, but I would bring you

berries, plums, if I knew
your thirst sunk deep as mine.

If I Could Shake

you like a mat from my floor,
pick you up and throw your dirt
out to a long wind, away.

But you have brushed each room of
my house with your scent, have touched
these walls with more than color.

Winds that flatten even boldest
trees could strike all this, right
to the foundation. And still

you would thrive underground,
a firm root, food I would need.
Even if all that were gone,

you would be here: every
one of the tunnels of my
body spills with your fruit.

Once

the scent of jasmine sifted
air, there was no moving

back, no turning from the sway
of stem, petal, trunk,

till neither of us could
stay upright. Leaning, dropping

to the softest grasses,
how strange that afterward

we simply rose. Was it
jasmine that blended us

into these intricate twinings?
And such a tiny blossom.

Sometimes

when I am whispering
to myself about you

as I go, leaves begin
to sound like your voice

as if that song could
settle into me, now.

Coloring

of the pond has turned reed brown,
yellow, red, orange, purple,
lavender where those ripples

slant under the indigo
of the shadows, clouds
pooling lilies in the cove

but already everything
has changed, sun shift, wind
clearing even memory.

You Standing

in a field of fallen
green apples. I am dreaming

this I believe. You are
upright above a sea of

dropped unripe fruit, looking
off as green mist lifts to

branches, twigs of the scarred
trees around you, as green air

opens, uncurls fronds, leaves
through the whole wood. You

have not yet moved among
these buds, this whispering.

Through

layers of rock the softer
dirt collects, fountains with moist
leaves of mint, scilla, purple
hyacinth, and primula.

*

Boundaries, margins, hedgerows.
Maintaining separate fields.
But the leaves, branches, white hair
of roots press beyond fences.

*

The clouds have woven countries.
Rain falls here and somewhere else
you might be moving, your feet
touching the same earth as mine.

Gift

The stone you handed me.
Oval as your face, palm

of your hand. How long
I have carried it with me.

That something so heavy
could help me rise.

So This

is what you saw. By
leaning down over
smooth stones around

the calm of the pond
I have seen my face.
And to think I was

worrying about
the flowers I would
wear when you find me.

In This Rain

it all comes back. Gentle
now. Your face, a mirror

of small rain drops. Blossoms
of these two dark trees by

the path, bursting petals.
Pink, white, and the darkness

of the inner flower
barely perceptible.

Even Rose Petals

fan out, away, yet still
touching till they drift

like blown rain to the ground
that drinks them in.

Maybe you have been closer
than I had thought,

across a crest
of another hill, just ripening.

Evening

lake's blue burnished, a long
quieting of ripples.
Entire gleam a mirror,
bronze gong, a deep bell
declaring. Is this you
beside me or a bough
almost brushing the dark?

Pine

needles yield to my feet, surface
crisp, soft underneath. From somewhere

I believe I can hear you come
this way, quiet, no announcement

other than the earth quivering,
the air filling clean with your scent.

The Return

will come when I least
expect it. Moon rise
into my field. Your
face, your brisk step on
my small estate. Calmed.
Bright body. Shadows
dissolved. The clearing.

We Are

no more outside the garden, or
inside fences, walls. Surfaces

dissolving. When I—or is it
you—look up, countless butterflies,

yellow flecks, little lights that pierce
the veil of what we thought was air,

dart, flutter, in, out of this
unlimited space we enter.

II

If a God

comes to you
a small
fish in the night,
simply
become water.

*

If a dove drifts
under your sheets
let him stay,
tuck his head
in a soft place,
rest, until
you are feathers.

*

He may come
as a lizard, a slip
of a green
slither across
your wall, crevices
left from past
freezes and thaws,
as he turns
translucent, persimmon,
ablaze.

*

Or a monkey,
who leaps
your crenelations.
Weightless

motion of silver-
brown fur, uncurling
tail, and keen
eyes focused
in, beyond.

*

When a god comes
to you as a man,
you will have no need
for questions, blossoms,
or bracelets.
Even a name.

About the Author

Wendy Barker is the author of three previous books of poetry, *Way of Whiteness, Let the Ice Speak,* and *Winter Chickens*; a chapbook, *Eve Remembers*; and a selection of poems accompanied by personal essays, *Poems' Progress*. Her translations (with Saranindranath Tagore), *Rabindranath Tagore: Final Poems*, received the Sourette Diehl Fraser Award for Literary Translation from the Texas Institute of Letters. As a scholar, she is the author of *Lunacy of Light: Emily Dickinson and the Experience of Metaphor*, as well as editor (with Sandra M. Gilbert) of *The House is Made of Poetry: The Art of Ruth Stone*. Recipient of NEA and Rockefeller fellowships as well as other awards in poetry, including the Mary Elinore Smith Poetry Prize from *The American Scholar*, her work has been translated into Hindi, Japanese, and Bulgarian. A Fulbright senior lecturer at the University of Sofia in 2000, she is a professor of English at the University of Texas at San Antonio.

Also by the Author

Poems' Progress

Rabindranath Tagore: Final Poems (translator, with
        Saranindranath Tagore)

Way of Whiteness: Poems

Eve Remembers (a chapbook)

The House is Made of Poetry: The Art of Ruth Stone (editor, with
        Sandra M. Gilbert)

Let the Ice Speak: Poems

Winter Chickens and Other Poems

Lunacy of Light: Emily Dickinson and the Experience of Metaphor

Cover photo: freestockphotos.com

Printed in the United States
36617LVS00009B/79